PETSYNC ®

GUIDE TO RESPONSIBLE DOG OWNERSHIP

VOLUME 1
DOG BITE PREVENTION

By Clark Brown

PETSYNC®

Guide to Responsible Dog Ownership

Volume 1: Dog Bite Prevention

All rights reserved

Copyright © 2016 by Clark Brown

ISBN: 978-0-692-68038-4

No part of this publication may be reproduced, stored in a retrieval system, or transmitted in any form or by any means electronic, mechanical, photocopying, recording, or otherwise, without the written permission of the author or publisher.

TABLE OF CONTENTS

OVERVIEW V

EPIDEMIOLOGY OF DOG BITES VII

TOPIC 1 - RESPONSIBILITIES OF A DOG OWNER 1

Lesson 1: A Dog Owner's Liability 1

    Instructional Objective 1

    Instructional Activity 1

    Conclusion 4

Lesson 2: What the Postal Service Wants You to Know 5

    Test Your Knowledge 7

Lesson 3: Leash Laws 8

    Test Your Knowledge 10

TOPIC 2 - FACTORS THAT INFLUENCE A DOG'S DISPOSITION 11

Lesson 1: Breed Alone Doesn't Determine a Dog's Temperament 11

    Instructional Activity: Sorting Exercise 11

TOPIC 3 - MEDICAL PREVENTION 15

Lesson 1: Reducing Aggression by Neutering or Spaying a Dog 15

    Instructional Objectives 15

    Instructional Activity: True/False Questions 15

Lesson 2: Rabies Vaccinations 18

    Test Your Knowledge 19

    Topic 1-3 Final Quiz 21

TOPIC 4 - SOCIALIZATION AND TRAINING 23

Lesson 1: Understanding a Dog's Body Language 23

    Instructional Objective 23

Lesson 2: Understanding Events Triggering A Dog's Aggression 26
   Instructional Objectives 26
   Instructional Activity 26
   Conclusion 27
   Multiple Choice Quiz 27

Lesson 3: Socializing Your Dog 29
   Instructional Activity: Role-Play Exercise 30

Lesson 5: The Owner's Leadership Role 35
   Instructional Objective 35
   Instructional Activity 35
   Topic 4 Section Quiz 38

TOPIC 5 - KEEPING YOUR DOG CONFINED 41

Lesson 1: Building a Dog Friendly Yard 41
   Instructional Objective 41

Lesson 2: Dog Proof Your Yard 44
   Instructional Activity 45

TOPIC 6 - WHAT TO DO WHEN YOUR DOG INJURES SOMEONE 47

Lesson 1: Actions to Take When Your Dog Bites a Person 47

Lesson 2: Creating a Dog Passport 49
   Instructional Activity: 49
   Topic 5 and 6 Final Quiz 50

Conclusion 52

Answer Key 53

ENDNOTES 63

OVERVIEW

No one wants to be bitten by an aggressive dog, and no one wants their family pet to injure an innocent person. This course provides the epidemiology and costs of dog bites, an overview of laws and penalties concerning dangerous animals, elements of responsible dog ownership, and safe practices, such as ways to prevent dog bites. In addition, you'll learn what to do if you or someone else is bitten by a dog, the actions to take if your dog bites another person, dog bite myths, and ways to ensure that your children interact safely with both your own and strange dogs.

Epidemiology of Dog Bites

Legal Responsibilities of a Dog Owner
- The Dog Owner's Potential Liability
- Leash Laws

What Shapes a Dog's Temperament?
- Factors that Influence a Dog's Disposition (heredity, training, socialization, health)

Medical Prevention
- Aggression Prevention through Neutering/Spaying
- Rabies Vaccination

Socialization and Training
- Understanding Your Dog's Body Language and Aggressive Triggers
- Reducing Aggressive Triggers Through Socialization
- The Owner's Leadership Role in Training a Well-Adjusted Dog

Keeping Your Dog Confined

- Strategies for Safe Pet Containment

When Your Dog Injures Someone

- Action Steps to Take When a Dog Is Involved in an Incident
- Dog Bite Myths

EPIDEMIOLOGY OF DOG BITES

Epidemiology is a long word that means the study of the patterns, causes, and effects of health and disease conditions in defined populations. In this case, it's the when, who, how often, and seriousness of dog bites.

If you watch the news, you may have the impression that dog bites are frightening but relatively rare events. You may be surprised to learn that the Center for Disease Control and prevention (the CDC) has reported that, on average, 4.5 million people in the United States suffer a dog bite for which they require medical attention every year. In fact, it's been estimated that half of the U.S. population will be bitten by a dog over the course of their lives.[1] Children are two times more likely to be bitten by a dog. And these are not feral strays encountered in the street; for the most part, they are familiar dogs.[2]

These animal encounters result in an enormous number of emergency room visits. In 2008 alone, approximately 316,000 people went to the emergency room seeking treatment for a dog bite. Further, roughly 9,500 of those visits resulted in admission to the hospital. The percentage of patients admitted to the hospital for dog bite was more than 3 times greater than those who came to the emergency room for treatment of other injuries.[3] These numbers only reflect the number of dog bites that were reported to either medical or law enforcement professionals; in fact, researchers believe that, roughly, only 17% of dog bites are reported.[4]

Who are the most likely victims? According to Dr. Jon Fraser, a member of the Texas Chapter of the American Academy of Pediatrics, by the time young people are seniors in high school, half of them will have been bitten by a dog. A study of dog bite incidents from 1979 to 2005 showed that victims younger than one year accounted for nearly 11% of the deaths and 56% were less than 10 years of age. In fact, nearly 30% of those who received fatal injuries were from 1 to 4 years old.[5] And the stature of a child who is bitten in comparison to an adult must be kept in mind. A dog that might bite an adult on the foot or leg can stand nearly eye-to-eye with a small child. It's easy to understand why, at Houston's Texas Children's Hospital, most of the patients who undergo reconstructive surgeries to treat dog bites are children who had been bitten on the face and experienced severe lacerations, infections, and scarring that could serve as a daily reminder for the rest of their lives.

It's important for you to be aware of which dogs are considered to be the most "dangerous," but it's also important to be aware that, although certain breeds receive a great deal of media attention, singling out one or two breeds is more than an injustice to those breeds; it can also blind you to the fact that all dogs are capable of aggressive behavior. And if communities, including property managers and landlords, put breed-specific (such as a pit bull-type dog, Rottweiler, and Doberman pinschers) restrictions in place, they ignore the smaller or seemingly docile dogs that may be just as much or even more of a problem.

While there are breeds that have been specifically bred to increase their aggressive tendencies, in addition to heredity, there are several other factors that play a role in the likelihood of a dog biting someone. One of the most important traits is the animal's sex: 80% of dogs found to be aggressive by veterinary professionals are unneutered males. In fact, a 2001 study by the American Veterinary Medical Association found that nearly 80% of dogs involved in dog bite incidents were "intact" males. In addition, a dog's early experiences in terms of training, socialization, abuse/neglect, health, and owner supervision also have key roles in determining that animal's tendency to bite.[6]

TOPIC 1
RESPONSIBILITIES OF A DOG OWNER

Lesson 1: A Dog Owner's Liability

Instructional Objective

Learners recognize that there are different types of legal theories that may render owners liable for injuries caused by their dogs, that they may be protected by homeowners or renters insurance, and that the insurers may have specific requirements.

Instructional Activity

Review the information below about a dog owner's legal responsibilities and potential liabilities and answer the series of multiple-choice questions that follow.

- In many states, dog owners are legally responsible for injuries caused by a dog regardless of their prior knowledge of their dog's propensity to bite. In these statutory liability states, the victim only needs to show that the victim was injured by the dog and that the dog belonged to the owner. The extent of recovery (e.g., all damages or only medical bills) and the type of injury necessary to recover (e.g., an actual bite or any other injury incurred in an attack) differ from state to state.

- Eighteen states follow the one-bite-rule where the victim has to prove that the owner kept a dog known to hurt people.

- Dog owners can also be liable for negligence if they failed to use reasonable care; for example, by allowing a dog to run off leash on a playground, or by permitting their dog to dig its way out of a yard without making any attempts to reinforce the fence.

- The exact laws differ by municipality and state. Dog owners should consult an attorney to determine how they could be held liable.

- Many homeowners and renter's insurance policies cover injuries caused by dogs. Some may have breed restrictions or require the dog to attend behavioral classes.

- Dog owners who bought insurance before they owned a dog should inform their carrier of their change in circumstances to ensure that they are covered for damages caused by their dog.

- Pet insurance only covers veterinary costs for a pet. It does not cover damages caused by a dog.

Multiple-choice Questions

1. *You live in a state that by statute holds dog owners liable for medical payments when a dog bites a person. If your child brings a friend to your house and your dog bites this child, you are*
    a) not responsible because your dog has never bitten anyone before
    b) not responsible because the dog was in your house and the child was only a visitor
    c) responsible because it only matters that the dog bit a person and that you own the dog
    d) responsible because every time a child gets hurt the owner is automatically responsible

Feedback: In a statutory liability state it only matters that you own the dog and that the dog bit someone. The victim does not have to prove that the owner had any knowledge that the dog had bitten anyone before. Even though the event took place in your home, you are still responsible. The child was an invited guest and not a trespasser. It is irrelevant that it was a child who was hurt. In this type of state, any time anyone is injured by a dog, the owner is responsible.

2. *You live in a statutory liability state and rescue a dog from a shelter. The dog had been abused and bit its previous owner. You are certain that you have rehabilitated the dog and let it run off leash in a town requiring dogs to be on a leash at all times. If the dog bites a person, you are liable because*

   a) you had previous knowledge of the dog's inclination to bite
   b) you were negligent because you let the dog off the leash in violation of the town's municipal law
   c) irrelevant of your prior knowledge, you are always responsible when your dog bites someone
   d) all of the above

Feedback: In a statutory liability state, the victim does not have to show that the owner knew of his or her dog's inclination to bite people. However, if the owner was aware that the dog was dangerous, the victim may seek additional compensation under the one-bite rule. Further, in many jurisdictions, the victim may also make a claim that the owner was negligent by not using reasonable care, such as walking the dog on a leash in public. This is especially true when the owner acted in violation of a local law, such as a leash ordinance.

3. *Your homeowner's insurance carrier requires notification when you add a dog to your household and charges more when the dog is a pit bull, Doberman pinscher, Rottweiler, or German shepherd. You decide not to tell your insurer about your new Rottweiler/shepherd mix puppy. Should the dog bite a letter carrier, the party responsible for paying any damages is*

   a) the insurance carrier because your insurance has a coverage clause for dog bites
   b) you because you didn't inform the insurance carrier
   c) the postal service because they are sending their employees into dangerous situations
   d) the letter carrier because he was trespassing

Feedback: It is your responsibility to comply with the homeowner's insurance requirements and inform the carrier that you own a dog. If you fail to let your insurance company know about the dog, they will deny coverage, and you will have to carry the cost of any litigation yourself. The letter carrier is not responsible since in his professional function he has an implied invitation to enter your property.

Conclusion

As a dog owner, you have a responsibility to educate yourself about dog-related laws in your town and state. You may also want to ensure that you have liability coverage in case your dog is involved in an aggressive incident. Insurance will help protect your assets and compensate anyone your dog may injure.

Here are some basic tips to prevent future incidents:

- Keep your dog on a leash when in public.

- If you let him out in the yard, make sure that he can't escape.

- Train and properly socialize your dog.

- If your dog acts territorial to strangers approaching your house, put the dog in another room while you answer the door.

Lesson 2: What the Postal Service Wants You to Know

If you knew that your next-door neighbor or someone on the next block owned a dog with a reputation for being aggressive, you would want to be sure that dog was controlled before you approached your neighbor's home. You probably wouldn't casually step into their yard or onto their front porch, certainly not five or six days a week. But every day, that's what mail carriers are forced to do as part of their job.

The American Veterinary Medical Association and the American Academy of Pediatrics have said that, in order, small children, the elderly, and mail carriers are most frequently the victims of dog bites.[7] In fact, in 2010, 5,669 postal employees were attacked by dogs. In 2014, Los Angeles, CA topped the list at 74 incidents. However, no city or town is exempt; these attacks occurred in more than 1,400 different locations.[8] And this costs more than the pain and suffering of the postal worker. If your dog bites a letter carrier, you will very likely pay their medical and other expenses, which can be thousands of dollars. In addition, the Postal Service must pay worker's compensation, legal fees, and the cost of carrier replacement, which costs them more than $25 million annually. Further, in some districts, mail service to a particular address can be interrupted if a carrier is injured or even threatened at that home and will be resumed only when the mailbox has been relocated to a safe area. Those are the reasons the U.S. Postal Service sponsors their annual Dog Bite Prevention Week, to protect themselves and other members of the communities they serve, including children, meter readers, and anyone else who may come in contact with an aggressive dog.

You may think that your dog "wouldn't hurt a fly," or "my dog doesn't bite"—two phrases frequently used to reassure letter carriers. In fact, many carriers who have been bitten reported that those were the owners' famous last words. Clearly, the statistics offered by the Postal Service indicate that dog owners are frequently mistaken, and they offer these tips to protect your mail carrier from dog bites (and yourself from legal problems and expensive restitution).

- Find out the usual time the carrier brings your mail.

- When the carrier is due, be sure that your dog is inside the house and keep it there until he or she has left.

- Before you open the door to accept a delivery, place the dog in another room with the door closed.

- If you have a mail slot, keep your dog away from it so they won't bite the mail carrier's fingers.

- If both your mailbox and your dog are inside a fenced yard, keep the dog on a leash and away from the mailbox during the time mail is usually delivered.

- Never walk up to the letter carrier to ask for your mail if your dog is outside.[9]

Test Your Knowledge.

4. According to the American Veterinary Medical Association and the American Academy of Pediatrics, who are the most frequent victims of aggressive dogs?

    a) Mail Carriers

    b) The elderly

    c) Adult family members

    d) Children

5. In 2014, which city had the highest number of dog bite incidents involving mail carriers?

    a) Los Angeles, CA

    b) Houston, TX

    c) Little Rock, AR

    d) Seattle, WA

6. Who assumes responsibility for medical bills and other expenses when a dog bites a mail carrier?

    a) The U.S. Postal Service

    b) The dog owner

    c) The mail carrier

    d) The Neighborhood Association

7. What can the Postal Service do if your dog threatens and/or bites a mail carrier?

    a) Discontinue delivery services until the situation is resolved

    b) Insist that the dog be destroyed

    c) Charge for delivery of the mail

    d) Talk to your neighbors about the problem

Lesson 3: Leash Laws

There is no one, clear law that governs the use of leashes. Some states don't insist that owners use leashes but do prohibit "at-large" dogs, which they define as being unaccompanied and off the owner's premises or not on a leash. Some locales require leashes in certain areas such as parks or during specific times of the day, for example, between sunset and sunrise. You should remember that even if you think you can control your dog off its leash, you're most likely still in violation of a leash law.

Two states, Michigan and Pennsylvania, do have leash laws: Michigan's is rather oddly written ("It shall be unlawful for any person for any owner to allow any dog . . . to stray unless held properly in leash."), while Pennsylvania's is very detailed, stating that "it is unlawful for the owner or keeper of any dog to fail to keep at all times the dog in any of the following manners," followed by "confined," "secured," "under the reasonable control of . . .," etc.[10]

Other states have no ordinances that directly require leashes, but do hold a person accompanied by a dog liable for any damage it does if it goes out of control. Mississippi, New York, Ohio, Oklahoma, Oregon, South Carolina, Virginia, and Wyoming, while having state laws regarding dogs at large, do give local governments the right to enact dog control ordinances.

The State of California does not have a leash law per say, but it does have very specific laws regarding dogs with the potential to be a danger to the community. California Food and Agricultural Code Division 14, Chapter 9 speaks to the question of these dogs in Sections 31601 to 31609:

"Potentially dangerous and vicious dogs have become a serious and widespread threat to the safety and welfare of citizens of this state. In recent years, they have assaulted without provocation and seriously injured numerous individuals, particularly children, and have killed numerous dogs. Many of these attacks have occurred in public places.

"The number and severity of these attacks are attributable to the failure of owners to register, confine, and properly control highly aggressive and potentially dangerous dogs. The necessity for the regulation and control of potentially dangerous and dogs known to attack people and other animals is a statewide problem, requiring statewide regulation, and existing laws are inadequate to deal with the threat to public health and safety posed by the pets of owners who haven't taken appropriate measures to ensure public safety.

The lawmakers go on to define terms such as "potentially dangerous dog," which is one that, "when unprovoked, on two separate occasions within the prior 36-month period, engages in any behavior that requires a defensive action by any person to prevent bodily injury when the person and the dog are off the property of the owner or keeper of the dog" or "any dog which, when unprovoked, bites a person causing a less severe injury." This law also covers unprovoked attacks on domestic animals that were not on the property of the dog's owner.

"Vicious" dogs are also defined, meaning "any dog seized under Section 599aa of the California Penal Code and upon the sustaining of a conviction of the owner or keeper under subdivision (a) of Section 597.5 of the California Penal Code," as well as any dog "which, when unprovoked, in an aggressive manner, inflicts severe injury on or kills a human being" or "any dog previously determined to be and currently listed as a potentially dangerous dog which, after its owner or keeper has been notified of this determination, continues the behavior." [11]

In some cities, both the length of the leash and the age at which a person can be considered to be responsible are outlined. In the City of Los Angeles, a dog must be on a leash that is no longer than 6 feet (including retractable leashes).

Test Your Knowledge.

8. A/an _____ dog is defined as one that is unaccompanied and off the owner's premises or not on a leash.

   a) Off-leash
   b) At-large
   c) Dangerous
   d) Vicious

9. Under California law, a potentially dangerous dog is one that engages in any behavior that requires a defensive action by any person to prevent bodily injury on _____ separate occasions within a _____ period.

   a) One, 24 month
   b) Two, 36 month
   c) Two, 12 month
   d) One, 36 month

10. In the City of Los Angeles, a dog must be on a leash that is no longer than _____

    a) 6 feet
    b) 10 feet
    c) 4 feet
    d) 5 feet

TOPIC 2
FACTORS THAT INFLUENCE A DOG'S DISPOSITION

Lesson 1: Breed Alone Doesn't Determine a Dog's Temperament

Several different factors influence a dog's behavior. A dog's breed is only one element. A dog's looks alone are an insufficient indicator of its propensity for aggression. A dog's potential to act aggressive is influenced by many factors, such as its heredity, early training, socialization, and health. Another important factor is how a person approaches a dog. A dog may act unexpectedly when it is afraid, territorial, in pain, touched in a way it doesn't like, or plays roughly.

Instructional Activity: Sorting Exercise

In this activity, you will first sort through a list of dogs of different breeds in the order of the threat level that you perceive the dogs to pose . Then sort a set of five dog descriptions below without any images associated with the descriptions, again in order of perceived threat. You will find the dogs breed matched with descriptions on the next page.

Maltese
Maltese are bred to be cuddly companion dogs. They are extremely lively and playful, and even as a Maltese ages, their energy level and playful demeanor remain fairly constant. Some Maltese may occasionally be snappish with smaller children and should be supervised when playing, although socializing them at a young age will reduce this habit. They also adore humans, and prefer to stay near them. [32] The Maltese is very active within a house, and, preferring enclosed spaces, does very well with small yards.

For this reason, the breed also fares well in apartments and townhouses, and is a prized pet of urban dwellers. [33] [34] Some Maltese may suffer from separation anxiety. [35]

Beagle

The Beagle has an even temper and gentle disposition. Described in several breed standards as "merry", they are amiable and typically neither aggressive nor timid, although this depends on the individual. They enjoy company, and although they may initially be standoffish with strangers, they are easily won over. They make poor guard dogs for this reason, although their tendency to bark or howl when confronted with the unfamiliar makes them good watch dogs. In a 1985 study conducted by Ben and Lynette Hart, the Beagle was given the highest excitability rating, along with the Yorkshire Terrier, Cairn Terrier, Miniature Schnauzer, West Highland White Terrier, and Fox Terrier [40] [c]

Rough Collie

Rough collies should show no nervousness or aggression, and are generally good with children and other animals.[6][7] However, they must be well socialized to prevent shyness. They are medium to large sized dogs, but can be well suited to live in small apartments because of their calm disposition. Like many herding dogs, collies can be fairly vocal, and some are difficult to train not to bark. The amount of herding instinct varies, with some dogs being quite drivey and others calmer.

Rough Collies are very loyal and may be one-family dogs (although most make exceptions for children), but are very rarely aggressive or protective beyond barking and providing a visual deterrent. They are typically excellent with children as long as they have been well-socialized and trained. They are eager to learn and respond best to a gentle hand

German Shepherd

German Shepherds are moderate active dogs and described in breed standards as self-assured. [11] The breed is marked by a willingness to learn and an eagerness to have a purpose. They are curious, which makes them excellent guard dogs and suitable for search missions. They can become over-protective of their family and territory, especially if not socialized correctly. They are not inclined to become immediate friends with strangers. [18] German Shepherds are highly intelligent and obedient. [19]

Rottweiler

This is a calm, confident, and courageous dog with a self-assured aloofness that does not lend itself to immediate and indiscriminate friendships. A Rottweiler is self-confident and responds quietly and with a wait-and-see attitude to influences in its environment. It has an inherent desire to protect home and family, and is an intelligent dog of extreme hardness and adaptability with a strong willingness to work, making them especially suited as a companion, guardian and general all-purpose dog. [16]

Dog Pictures and Bios

(The dogs are sorted in order of posing the greatest to least threat)

1. *This dog is very territorial and has snapped at children before.*
2. *This dog has been abused by his owner. It is distrustful and can often be found tied up in the yard.*
3. *This dog is left alone a lot. It is fearful of strangers.*
4. *This dog is part of a family with five children. He is well socialized and calm even when the surroundings are sometimes a little chaotic.*
5. *This dog comes from a long line of service dogs and is currently working as a guide dog for a blind neighbor.*

1. Maltese   **2. Beagle**   **3. Rough Collie**   **4. German Shepherd**   **5. Rottweiler**

TOPIC 3
MEDICAL PREVENTION

Lesson 1: Reducing Aggression by Neutering or Spaying a Dog

The best time to neuter a dog is before he is six months old. Neutering a dog will eliminate testosterone-related, aggressive behavior, including the following:

- roaming

- marking territory

- dominant behavior over other dogs

Neutering a dog is also an important method to controlling the dog population. When dogs produce unwanted offspring, the pups will end up in animal shelters where about 4 million dogs and cats are euthanized every year.

Instructional Objectives

Learners will understand how neutering a dog reduces potentially aggressive behavior.

Instructional Activity: True/False Questions

Learners will answer a series of true/false questions using the information on the following page.

Early Neutering of a Male Dog—Behavior Changes

- **Marking territory**: A neutered dog does not feel the need to alert other dogs to its presence by frequently urinating in its surroundings.

- **Roaming**: Intact dogs often leave to search for female dogs in heat. Neutering the dog will eliminate or lessen this urge.

- **Dominance over other dogs**: A neutered dog does not fight with other dogs over a female dog in heat. Aggressive behavior related to this need is eliminated in a neutered dog.

- **Inappropriate mounting**: Neutering eliminates or greatly reduces sexually motivated mounting.

- Intact male dogs are responsible for 80% of all dog attacks.

Early Spaying of a Female Dog—Behavior Changes

- **Marking**: Female dogs in heat mark their surroundings to attract male dogs. Spaying eliminates this behavior and will also stop the bloody discharge that occurs during a heat cycle.

- **Roaming:** Once spayed, female dogs will not try to escape to mate with a male.

- **Irritability**: The hormonal changes of a heat cycle make female dogs irritable and may cause them pain. A spayed female's behavior will be more regular.

- **Aggression**: Spaying will lessen aggressive behaviors that are based on a need to fight for a male dog's attention. Further, females will not experience a false pregnancy, causing them to adopt guarding behavior that is directed towards objects that are treated like puppies.

Most importantly, a spayed female cannot get pregnant with unwanted puppies.

Neutering or spaying a dog only eliminates aggressive behavior that is caused by high testosterone levels or the female dog's heat cycle. Aggressive behavior due to fear or territorial behavior needs to be controlled through training and socialization.

True/False Questions

Spaying or neutering my dog will

11. reduce its need to try to escape in order to mate
    True_____   False_____

12. eliminate all types of aggressive behavior
    True_____   False_____

13. make my dog a better behaved pet
    True_____   False_____

14. increase its need to urinate and mark everything
    True_____   False_____

Lesson 2: Rabies Vaccinations

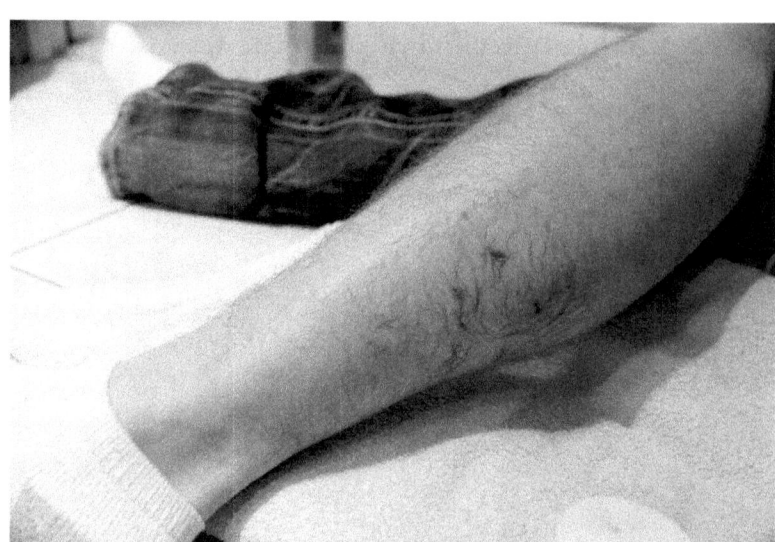

Rabies is a vaccine-preventable disease, for both humans and animals. Worldwide, domestic dogs are the most common source of human infection. However, this threat has largely been abated in the United States by dog vaccination programs, and bats are now considered of greatest risk of transmitting the infection to humans. Human rabies infections in the United States are rare, with 34 cases occurring since 2003 and only 24 of them acquired domestically.

Although there is an effective vaccine to prevent rabies infection, more than 55,000 people die from rabies each year around the world. Preventative human rabies vaccines are expensive, and generally only given to those in high-risk professions or situations. The best prevention method is avoiding contact with unknown or wild animals. Pets should be kept under supervision and regularly vaccinated by a veterinarian, and individuals should not touch or interfere with wildlife. After possible exposure and following all animal bites, individuals should seek medical attention immediately. Per California's health and safety code, dogs must be vaccinated at 3 months of age and revaccinated one year after the primary immunization with an approved type rabies vaccine. Dogs shall be revaccinated thereafter at least every three years with an approved type of rabies vaccine.

Test Your Knowledge.

15. *Worldwide, bats are the most common source of human infection.*

    True_____   False_____

16. *In 2003, there were 52 rabies cases in the United States.*

    True_____   False_____

17. *Per California's health and safety code, dogs must be vaccinated at ___ months of age.*

    True_____   False_____

Topic 1-3 Final Quiz

18. If a dog injures another person, the dog owner could be liable

    a) just because he is the owner and the dog bit someone under a state with statutory liability laws

    b) if he had previous knowledge of the dog's propensity to bite

    c) if he was negligent, for example by letting the dog off leash in a public place

    d) all of the above

19. People most likely to be bit are

    a) dog owners

    b) children

    c) Postal Carriers

    d) Veterinarians

20. One very basic way to prevent dog bites is to

    a) keep a dog on a leash when in public

    b) visit dog parks so the dog gets too tired to become aggressive

    c) only get a dog that is of a calm breed

    d) keep the dog in the house at all times

21. A dog's temperament is determined by

    a) breed

    b) genetics

    c) training and socialization

    d) a combination of breed, genetics, training, and socialization

22. *Aside from being a legal requirement, rabies vaccinations also*

   a) calm down the dog

   b) protect people and the dog if it is bitten by a rabid animal

   c) help in the dog's socialization

   d) repel wild animals who have rabies

23. *Neutering or spaying a dog is a good idea because it*

   a) controls aggressive behavior that is caused by the dog's need to mate

   b) reduces its willingness to roam to find a mate

   c) reduces its need to urinate to advertise its presence

   d) all of the above

TOPIC 4
SOCIALIZATION AND TRAINING

Lesson 1: Understanding a Dog's Body Language

Instructional Objective

This activity will familiarize learners with the body language of a dog. Learners will be able to identify whether a dog's body language indicates that the dog is upset and about to become aggressive or relaxed and happy.

1. **Mouth**

   Friendly dog: mouth open and relaxed
   Tense dog: mouth closed, lips retracted exposing teeth, muzzle wrinkled
   Anxious dog: mouth closed, lips slightly retracted exposing front teeth, nervously licking lips

Feedback: When a dog is friendly, its whole body is relaxed. The mouth is closed or slightly open, with the lips relaxed. A dog that may act aggressively will have its mouth closed and its lips pulled back, displaying its teeth. Its muzzle, the area below the eyes that contains the nose and mouth, is wrinkled. Some anxious dogs will give you a "submissive grin" that exposes only the front teeth or show displacement behavior like nervously licking its lips or yawning exaggeratedly.

2. **Eyes**

   Friendly dog: Eyes are normal-shaped, round, or sometimes almond-shaped
   Tense dog: Eyes appear larger than normal and are staring directly at the viewer with a tense facial expression

Anxious dog: Eyes are averted and/or the whites of the eyes are showing (half-moon eyes)

Feedback: The eyes of a happy dog are relaxed and normal shaped. When a dog is tense, its eyes may appear enlarged. If it is contemplating aggression, the dog may stare directly at you with a tense facial expression. An anxious dog will avert its gaze and the whites of the eyes will show in a half-moon shape. This is a dog's equivalent of clenching its fists.

3. Ears

   Friendly dog: Ears are relaxed and held naturally
   Tense dog: Ears are up and forward
   Anxious dog: Ears are back and flattened

Feedback: A relaxed dog will have his ears in their natural position. When a dog is about to become aggressive, the ears are forward and up. A dog that is afraid will have its ears flattened to the sides of its head.

4. Tail

   Friendly dog: Tail is in a natural position, may wag side to side gently
   Tense dog: Tail is held still in a high position
   Anxious dog: Tail tucked between its legs

Feedback: A happy dog will hold its tail in a natural position and may wag it gently side to side. If the dog is afraid, the tail may be in a low position or even tucked between its legs. A dog about to become aggressive will hold the tail in a high position without motion, or only rigid motion.

5. Hair

   Friendly dog: Coat lies flat
   Tense dog: Hair along the spine is raised
   Anxious dog: Suddenly starts shedding

Feedback: When a dog is on high alert, it may raise its hair along the spine. This is similar to people experiencing goose bumps. An anxious dog will suddenly start shedding its coat.

6. Body

Friendly dog: Weight is evenly distributed across all four legs
Tense dog: Weight is slightly forward with toes curled into the ground
Anxious dog: Hunched, cowered closer to the floor, trying to look small

Feedback: The body of a dog that is tense is rigid, with the weight distributed toward the front legs. When a dog is relaxed, the weight is distributed evenly, and the dog is moving its body playfully. An anxious dog will try to make itself look small by looking hunched or cowering on the floor.

Lesson 2: Understanding Events Triggering A Dog's Aggression

Instructional Objectives

Familiarize yourself with the different triggers that can cause a dog to react aggressively and identify situations that may cause this type of behavior.

Instructional Activity

Definitions and Multiple Choice Questions

Territorial

A dog considers its home and yard, its toys, food, and sometimes its people its territory. When a dog guards this territory, it will display tense and sometimes aggressive behavior.

Unwanted Handling

A dog, much like people, doesn't always want to be touched and handled. Depending on the dog's previous experiences, pulling and poking the dog could make it annoyed, afraid, and/or feel challenged.

Fear

When a dog is afraid, it does not really want to engage with you, but if it feels that the situation is becoming more threatening, the dog will defend itself and that defense could include biting.

Rough Play

When you play tug-of-war or another rough game with a dog, you are challenging it, perhaps giving it a shot at dominance over you should you lose, and encouraging guarding and assertive behavior. This assertive behavior can be expressed in growling, snapping, and even biting. Your dog could become so excited by the play that it cannot tell the difference between the toy you are pulling and the hand that is holding it. Rough play fosters the type of aggressive behavior that you would seek to discourage in a well-socialized dog.

Conclusion

"Becoming familiar with your dog's body language and triggers will help you understand when your dog may become dangerous to you and people around the dog. It will also assist in training and socializing your dog to help him become calm and well adjusted."

Multiple Choice Quiz

24. *In which of these situations is the dog acting in a territorial manner:*
    a) The dog growls at you when you move its food bowl away while it is eating
    b) You walk by a house and a dog runs up to the fence and barks at you
    c) Your friend's dog growls at you when you are lifting up her infant son
    d) All of the above

25. *Which one of these situations exemplifies <u>proper</u> handling?*
    a) A person sneaks up on the dog from behind and pulls its ears
    b) A person approaches the dog from the front, lets it sniff his hand, and pets him on the back
    c) A person yanks a dog by its collar
    d) A person making loud noises runs up to the dog and tries to pet it

26. *Which of these situations could make a dog afraid?*
    a) Being in new surroundings with people it doesn't know
    b) A visit to the vet
    c) Loud construction work in front of the house
    d) All of the above

27. Which one of these situations are examples of rough play?

    a) Letting the dog grab your sleeve with its mouth and tugging it back and forth
    b) Wrestling with the dog on the floor
    c) Playing tug-of-war with a toy
    d) All of the above

Lesson 3: Socializing Your Dog

Socializing a dog means to help the dog become adjusted to the human world and its sights and sounds.

The easiest time to socialize a dog is during the puppy stage, from 3 to 12 weeks old. From 12 to 18 weeks of age, it becomes more challenging to socialize your dog. Even after this age you can still socialize your dog, but it may take a little longer for the dog to overcome fears acquired during its early weeks. If in the course of socializing your dog you find that it still seems unreasonably anxious, you may want to consult with a Dog Trainer or Applied Behaviorist that has experience addressing aggression issues.

Dogs should get used to the following:

People: Dogs should meet people of all sizes and ethnicities, in uniforms, carrying objects, children, people in wheelchairs, etc. Ideally they should meet five new people a day. Each encounter should be positive. The new people the dog meets should speak in a "happy" voice, pet the dog gently, and perhaps give it a treat.

Sounds: Dogs also need to be sensitized to sounds of all kinds, including construction noises, children playing, traffic noises, television, the vacuum cleaner, fire engines, etc. If a dog is fearful of a particular sound, play a recording of the sound at low volume and speak in a "happy" voice to your dog. As the dog becomes less fearful of the sound, turn up the volume.

Objects: Dogs may act afraid around a particular object, such as a vacuum cleaner, an umbrella, a television, or a car. Slowly introduce the dog to the object, speaking in a "happy" voice and rewarding the dog with a treat if it relaxes around the object. Place a favorite toy next to the object, or create a trail of treats to entice the dog to come up to the object.

Environments: A dog may be afraid in certain environments, such as a veterinarian's office or a dog groomer. Visit the environment with the dog, have it meet the people there, and perhaps feed it a treat. The intent is for the dog to associate the place with positive interactions.

Don't:
- Overload your dog with new impressions. Use a stepped approach; introduce your dog to a small group before you bring it into a large group.

- React to its fear with coddling; otherwise, it will connect fearful reactions with a "reward."

- Speak to it soothingly when it is acting fearful. This will reward the dog's anxiety. Act upbeat and happy instead.

Do:
- Reward your dog for desirable behavior.

- Interact with your dog as much as possible.

- Consider a puppy kindergarten and obedience class to socialize your dog with other dogs and owners and learn how better to communicate with your dog.

Instructional Activity: Role-Play Exercise

In this exercise, learners are the owners of different dogs that are going through socialization. Their task is to select the appropriate strategy to socialize the dog to a person, object, or sound.

Socialization to People

Coco is not used to the letter carrier yet. To help her overcome her hesitation you should

a) feed her treats when the letter carrier arrives and stop when he leaves

b) ignore Coco

Feedback: a) You want Coco to make a positive association with the letter carrier. Feeding her treats while the letter carrier is present and immediately stopping when the letter carrier is gone helps Coco make the connection that good things happen when the mail arrives. If you ignore Coco's timidity, it could blossom into a full fear of the mail carrier.

Coco doesn't try and hide when the mail arrives anymore but still doesn't trust the letter carrier completely. You should

a) with his consent, ask the letter carrier to hold out Coco's favorite treat for her

b) ask the letter carrier to come inside and hold Coco on his lap

Feedback: a) Coco needs to come to terms with the letter carrier on her own. Holding a treat out for her may entice her to come closer to the letter carrier and make a positive association with the person. If you just have the mail person pick up Coco, you may get the opposite reaction and make her more fearful because she is not ready to be handled by someone who still makes her nervous.

Coco is finally ready to greet the letter carrier calmly. You should

a) ignore Coco, happy to cross this task off your list

b) praise Coco and use an upbeat voice to reinforce that seeing the letter carrier is a happy occasion

Feedback: b) You always want to acknowledge and praise desirable behavior, especially since Coco worked so hard to overcome her trepidation. If you ignore her achievement, Coco will not make the positive connection and may not be motivated to continue to greet the letter carrier.

Socialization to Objects

Rusty is nervous about a large houseplant in the house and is hiding under the couch. To help him get over his nervousness you should

a) give him a treat while he is hiding under the couch

b) put a treat halfway between Rusty and the offending plant

Feedback: b) It is best to coax Rusty out of his hiding place by putting a treat close to the thing that is scaring the dog. The goal is to have him associate the plant with a positive experience. By feeding him a treat while he is still under the couch, he associates hiding with getting a treat, which reinforces the wrong behavior.

Rusty is coming out of the hiding place for his treat, which is close to the scary plant. Should you say

a) "It's okay, Rusty" in an anxious voice

b) "Good Boy" in an upbeat, happy voice

Feedback: b) You want to speak with your dog using an upbeat, happy tone. If you speak in an anxious voice, Rusty will believe that there is something terribly wrong with that plant.

Rusty is following your trail of treats to the houseplant and stops a few feet away from it. To help him overcome his fear, you should

a) pick him up and have him finally confront the plant

b) try to coax him closer with the ultimate treat or his favorite toy using a happy voice

Feedback: b) Rusty needs to meet the enemy plant on his own terms. If you force the confrontation, you could reinforce his fear. It is best to be patient with him and continue to make meeting the plant a happy, positive experience.

Socialization to Sounds

Pebbles does not like the sound of lawn mowers. You should

a) make a different loud noise to distract her from the lawn mower

b) have her listen to the lawn mower from a distance where it is not so loud

Feedback: b) When trying to socialize your dog to a new sound that makes her uncomfortable, have her get used to a quieter version of the sound first. Make it a positive experience by playing with her and her favorite toy or feeding her treats while she listens to the sound.

Pebbles is okay when she hears a lawn mower at a distance, but she still hides in the basement when the lawn mower is on her lawn. You should

a) speak to her in a soothing voice when she is hiding

b) have her listen to a recording of the lawn mower and increase the volume slightly every time she is comfortable with the previous setting

Feedback: b) You don't want to coddle Pebbles when she is anxious and reinforce that behavior. Instead, help her get used to the sound very gradually and make it a pleasant experience by feeding her treats or playing with her while the sound plays in the background.

Pebbles is relaxed when she listens to the recording but has yet to experience a real lawn mower without fear. You should

a) turn on the recording of the lawn mower sound and play with Pebbles right before the gardener arrives, then try and see whether the sound of the real lawn mower still disturbs her when mixed with the sound of the recorded lawn mower

b) take Pebbles outside on a tight leash because now she is ready for the real thing

Feedback: a) Pebbles' encounter with the lawn mower should take place in a happy, non-threatening way. If she is forced to deal with the noise while on a short leash that affords her no possibility of a getaway, it will only reinforce her fears.

Proper socialization is essential in training a dog to be calm and non-aggressive around people, objects, and sounds. The more comfortable a dog is in human society, the less likely it is for the dog to be part of a situation as a fearful aggressor.

Lesson 5: The Owner's Leadership Role

Instructional Objective

In addition to socializing their dogs, owners are also responsible for asserting themselves as leaders in their relationships with their dogs. Assertive, calm leadership is a pre-requisite for successful training and behavior modification. This type of relationship allows a dog to be calm and non-aggressive in its interactions with people.

Instructional Activity:

Learners are presented with a series of situations where they have to remove a dog from a dominant into a submissive position, using information presented in the material below.

My Human, the Pack Leader

Dogs are pack animals that live in groups and require a strong, calm, and assertive leader in order to feel relaxed and secure. It is important for dogs to feel that the hierarchy in which they live is stable and that they can rely on their leader to make the decisions for them.

In a human-dog relationship, the dog must always perceive the human as the pack leader regardless of whether the person is an eight-year-old girl or a thirty-year-old man. It is the human's responsibility to maintain the order. If a dog perceives a power vacuum, it will step in. In the dog's mind, this action would be for the good of the pack. This does not mean that the dog would enjoy being the leader. Trying to keep a bunch of unruly humans in line is severely stressful to the dog and will result in dominant aggressive behavior. In short, to make a dog's life easy and keep it happy and content, the owner must take the lead and set the rules.

Setting the rules means that the leader—i.e., the owner—decides when it is time to eat, play, or walk. As leaders, humans eat first, sleep in the most comfortable spot, and own all the toys. In daily life that translates into not letting a dog walk ahead of you and not allowing the dog to walk through a door or up the stairs before you do. The dog should not initiate play time—only the leader is allowed to do that. Since the leader owns all the toys, pick out one or two toys for the dog to play with and put them away again when play time is over. At meal times, make sure that the dog sees you eat first before it is allowed to eat. Acting like this is not mean to the dog, rather, it reassures it of its place in the pack and helps it feel calm and secure.

On a daily basis, and especially if your dog does not wait for your command to act, practice your obedience commands such as "sit," "wait," or "come" before you engage in a pleasurable interaction like going for a walk or having some play time. Always correct undesirable behavior immediately by removing attention from the dog or giving it a time out. An example for removing attention is turning and walking away from a dog that jumps on you to greet you.

You are responsible for making your dog act calm and non-aggressive. You must take on your leadership role in order to keep your dog and everyone in your environment safe. You and your dog may also benefit from formal sessions with a dog trainer to help you solidify this relationship.

Exercise

Situation 1
The dog is sleeping on the bed with its head on the pillow. Next to the bed is a dog bed.

Feedback: The leader of the pack always sleeps in the most comfortable spot. Allowing your dog to sleep in the bed, especially at the top of the bed, lets it believe that it is at least your equal if not more dominant than you. It is best to let it sleep on the dog bed next to you.

Situation 2
The dog, carrying a toy in its mouth, approaches the owner who is working at the desk.

Feedback: Even though it is cute when your dog comes up to you with a toy, you cannot play with it at that moment. If you do, the dog believes that you follow its commands, not the other way around. Put the toy away and play with your dog later, at a time you determine.

Situation 3

The dog runs ahead of the owner when they are out for a walk and pulls on the leash.

Feedback: As the pack leader, you must be in the **lead**. You decide where and when to walk. By walking ahead of you, your dog is not happily investigating the neighborhood; it is trying to migrate in a manner that will keep the pack safe since you are not doing your job as a leader. To keep your dog calm, you need to maintain the lead.

Topic 4 Section Quiz

28. A dog displaying a closed mouth revealing the front teeth, with half-moon eyes, ears laid back against its head, its tail between its legs, and a cowering body posture is most likely feeling

    a) friendly

    b) angry

    c) anxious

29. An anxious dog is

    a) dangerous because it could become so fearful that it decides to defend itself and bites the source of its fear

    b) safe because it is too scared to do anything

    c) a good pack leader because it will make all decisions in a calm manner

30. When an unknown person runs up to a dog and makes loud noises, the dog will feel

    a) annoyed

    b) anxious

    c) challenged

    d) all of the above

31. The best time to socialize a dog is when it is

    a) 3-12 weeks old because the dog is willing to accept new experiences

    b) 4-6 months old after it's received all its vaccinations

    c) fully grown because it is less distractible than a puppy

32. When you socialize a dog you should

   a) immediately expose it to the whole of human society; dogs are resilient and can handle large crowds

   b) gradually, but steadily introduce the dog to new sounds, objects, and people

   c) keep it mostly at home because otherwise it will become too anxious

33. A dog questions your position as pack leader when

   a) it growls when you remove its food bowl

   b) charges through the door before you go

   c) bumps your hand while you are having dinner to get something to eat

   d) all of the above

34. When a person is the pack leader, the dog is

   a) resentful because the dog wants this position of power

   b) sad because it has to do what you tell it to

   c) calm because it knows its place in the hierarchy and is happy to follow your lead

TOPIC 5
KEEPING YOUR DOG CONFINED

Lesson 1: Building a Dog Friendly Yard

Instructional Objective

During this exercise you will be introduced to the proper way to confine a dog in a yard. Given a scenario, you will identify the proper modification to keep a yard dog friendly and the dog confined. Fictional characters **Lisa, Paul,** and **Tucker** will be used to give you a better understanding of the scenarios.

Setting

Lisa picks up Paul and Tucker to go to the dog park. During their walk, Paul tells Lisa that he's thinking of letting Tucker spend the summer in the yard because he believes that is a more natural environment for his dog and maybe Tucker will get more exercise this way.

Lisa warns Paul that while it is nice for Tucker to have an additional space to go to, putting the dog in the yard will not replace walking and interacting with him for the following reasons:

- As a pack animal, Tucker needs companionship. Leaving him in the yard by himself all day long will make him just as bored and lonely as if he were locked up in the house by himself.

- Being outdoors does not replace the exercise and mental stimulation Tucker gets from being walked at least twice a day.

- A bored dog will be more likely to want to escape the confines of a yard. And once he escapes, he can become hurt, cause accidents, or scare people.

Paul argues that there are a lot of dogs that stay out in yards and seem happy. Lisa explains that creating an outdoor space for Tucker is fine, but it can't replace the daily interaction Paul has with him now.

Lisa then emphasizes that if Tucker is allowed to go out in the yard, Paul has to create the proper confinement for him so he doesn't escape. As they continue their walk, Lisa points out the different methods their neighbors have used to reinforce their yards for their dogs.

Below is a list of common confinement scenarios and suggested solutions.

Scenario 1: Yard with a chain link fence enclosure where a dog is trying to dig its way out at one end, while at the other end, a laborer fills a trench under the fence with concrete.

Feedback 1: If your dog likes to dig out, fill a 1-foot deep trench under your fence with ready mix concrete to create a barrier.

Scenario 2: Yard with picket fence enclosure showing a dog jumping up on the fence while the homeowner is installing 45-degree extensions on top of the fence.

Feedback 2: Stop a dog from jumping over a fence by installing chain link or wire extensions on top of an existing fence.

Scenario 3: Small dog trying to push through the ornamental opening in a wrought iron fence while homeowner installs livestock fencing across the fence.

Feedback 3: Use livestock fencing to deter dogs from putting their heads and bodies through wrought iron. Don't use chicken wire—it can injure the dog.

Scenario 4: Yard with masonry block wall enclosure. Dog has two paws on top of the enclosure. Homeowner using drill to attach decorative metal sheeting on top.

Feedback 4: When a dog is able to jump on top of a block wall fence and pull himself over the top, place linoleum or metal sheeting on top to eliminate traction for the dog's paws.

Scenario 5: Dog owner with a shady, properly enclosed yard bringing dog fresh water followed by a child with dog toys.

Feedback 5: If you decide to keep your pet in a properly confined outdoor space, you also need to ensure that there is sufficient shade, protection from the elements (hot and cold weather), and fresh water available. You should also provide some toys to relieve boredom.

Lesson 2: Dog Proof Your Yard

Enclosure

Chain Link Fence

A chain link fence is a good choice for an enclosure system, especially if it has been reinforced with a concrete trench to prevent digging out and wire extensions that may be necessary to stop your dog from jumping over the fence.

Wrought Iron Fence

A wrought iron fence can be further reinforced with livestock wire to prevent your dog from squeezing through the opening. Don't use poultry wire, as it can injure the dog. In addition, you may need to reinforce the enclosure further by adding a concrete trench so your dog can't dig out and wire extensions if your dog is a jumper.

Block Wall

With this fence, you may need to add either some sheeting on top of the fence to prevent your dog from gaining enough traction to jump over the enclosure or an extension that cannot be jumped.

Wood Fencing

Wood fencing (dog-eared) generally comes in 6-foot vertical sections. Purchasing 8-foot sections (use treated lumber only) would allow a 1-foot section below ground for diggers and an extra 1-foot for jumpers. If you go with 6-foot sections, you might also consider adding a chain link extension at the top of the fence.

Shelter

A dog that is kept in the yard needs some shelter that provides shade and protects it from the cold or extreme heat. If you set up a kennel in the yard, make sure that it has a roof cover.

Water

It is important to give your dog access to fresh water at all times. The water should be in a bowl that your dog cannot tip over.

Toys

Leave some toys in the yard for your dog so it won't get bored when left alone. Equipped with the information from the previous exercise, create your own pet containment system.

Instructional Activity

Below, you are presented with an open yard and different options for fencing, pet containment, shelter, water, and toys. Circle the items needed to create a safe confined environment.

Elements to Create the Yard

Fencing
- Chain-link Fence
- Wrought Iron Fence
- Block Wall Fence
- Wood

Confining Reinforcements
- Concrete
- Wire Extensions
- Linoleum Sheeting
- Livestock Wire

Shelter
- Dog House
- Kennel
- Kennel Roof Cover

Water
- Large bowl or bucket
- Weighted water bowl

Toys
- Squeaky toys
- Treat balls
- Chew toys

TOPIC 6
WHAT TO DO WHEN YOUR DOG INJURES SOMEONE

Lesson 1: Actions to Take When Your Dog Bites a Person

Multiple Choice Questions

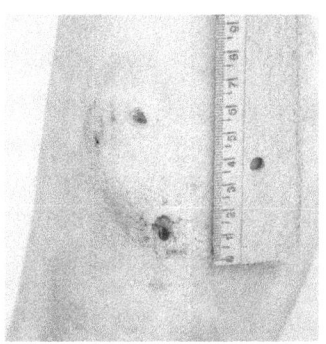

Below is a list of the proper procedures dog owners should follow when they find themselves in a situation where their dog bites or otherwise injures someone.

35. *What is the first thing you should do when your dog attacks or injures someone?*

   a) Call 911
   b) Pull the victim away from your dog
   c) Pull your dog away from the victim and confine it if possible
   d) Pretend it's not your dog

Feedback: The first thing you need to do is to remove and secure your dog so it can't further injure the victim or hurt anyone else.

36. *Once you've removed your dog, what should you do next?*

   a) Call your vet to check on your dog's rabies information
   b) Assist the victim and contact emergency services if necessary
   c) Check on your dog to make sure it's okay
   d) Call your insurance agent

Feedback: Before you do anything else you have to assist the victim. Depending on the severity of the injury, the victim may need an ambulance.

37. *What information should you give to the victim?*
    a) Your name, address, and contact information
    b) Your dog's rabies vaccination date and dog license number
    c) Your veterinarian's information
    d) All of the above

Feedback: You should always have all of this information readily available. If there were any witnesses to the incident, you should also get their contact information.

The 10-day-quarantine rule. Many jurisdictions require a dog that bites a person to be quarantined for 10 days in order to determine whether the dog has rabies. This applies whether or not the dog was vaccinated. If your dog bites someone, you should voluntarily adhere to this rule.

Lesson 2: Creating a Dog Passport

This activity reinforces the importance of keeping your dog's information with you and suggests easy ways of accomplishing this task.

Instructional Activity:

Review the information you may need to have available should you become involved in a dog attack. Write your own information on an index card. Once all the fields of the card are completed, stick it in your wallet for future reference.

Sample Dog and Owner Data

Owner's Name: Paul Miller
Address: 409 State Street, South Bay, CA
Phone Number: (408)719-4567
Dog's Name: Tucker
Dog's License Numbers: 82 934
Town Issuing License: South Bay
Date of Last Rabies Vaccination: 03/28/13
Veterinarian's Name: Bay Ridge Animal Hospital, Dr. Hamilton
Veterinarian's Address: 55 5th Avenue, South Bay, CA
Veterinarian's Phone Number: (408)755-4321

Topic 5 and 6 Final Quiz

True/False Questions

38. *To keep a dog from escaping it is best to have it chained in the yard.*

    True_____   False_____

39. *The only thing a dog needs in a yard is shade.*

    True_____   False_____

40. *There should always be fresh water available to a dog kept outdoors.*

    True_____   False_____

Multiple Choice

41. *The 10-day quarantine rule means*

    a) when you first bring a dog home it has to stay indoors for 10 days

    b) after a rabies vaccination, a dog has to stay home for 10 days

    c) if a dog bites someone, it has to be quarantined for 10 days to determine whether it has rabies

    d) after receiving your application for a dog license, it takes 10 days for the license to be issued

Sequencing

Put these steps in the right order.

When your dog is involved in a dog attack and injures a person, you should

- assist the victim___

- provide your personal information and your dog's information___

- remove your dog and confine it___

- gather the names and numbers of any witnesses___

Dog Bite Myths

While there are several facts about dog bites that are generally well known, such as not petting a strange dog and that a dog who is wagging his tail is not always friendly, there are also many myths that the public accepts as the truth. If you do, you could get yourself into trouble, whether not you're a dog owner or just a person strolling through the local park.

The first is that a "good" dog can be trusted not to bite unless they are threatened. The fact that the majority of dog bite victims are children between the ages of 5 and 9 disproves this one. How about the idea that good family dogs are unlikely to bite strangers? Unfortunately, dogs that are fine with even the youngest members of your family may react badly to outsiders, particularly if they're not accustomed to unfamiliar people. And dog bites are just as likely to carry risks of disease and infection as cat bites. Although their teeth may not puncture flesh the way that a cat's teeth do, they have much stronger jaws and their bites can crush flesh. Such wounds are much more likely to become infected.[12]

Conclusion

There's no question that a dog can add a great deal to your life, whether you live alone or in a large family. There's a reason that they're called man's best friend. However, although it's tempting to think of them as being "almost human," they are not short people in fur suits; they're animals, and animals can be unpredictable.

Owning a dog is a responsibility that can extend over many years, from the day you bring home that adorable puppy until your dog's last days. You've learned a great deal in this course, but there's always more to know.

The websites of the American Veterinary Medical Association and the Humane Society of the United States offer an enormous amount of information on every aspect of dog ownership during every stage of your dog's life, from choosing the perfect breed to feeding to training to having fun with your dog. There are also many excellent books on the subject. Some of the best are *How to Raise the Perfect Dog: Through Puppyhood and Beyond*, written by Cesar Millan and Melissa Jo Peltier, and *How to Be Your Dog's Best Friend*, by the monks of New Skeet.

Learn all that you can and enjoy your wonderful and loving pet, but always remember to keep it, your family, and the community safe.

Clark Brown

ANSWER KEY

Topic 1 / Lesson 1

1. *You live in a state that by statute holds dog owners liable for medical payments when a dog bites a person. If your child brings a friend to your house and your dog bites this child, you are*

    c) Responsible because it only matters that the dog bit a person and that you own the dog.

2. *You live in a statutory liability state and rescue a dog from a shelter. The dog had been abused and bit its previous owner. You are certain that you have rehabilitated the dog and let it run off leash in a town requiring dogs to be on a leash at all times. If the dog bites a person, you are liable because*

    d) all of the above

3. *Your homeowner's insurance carrier requires notification when you add a dog to your household and charges more when the dog is a pit bull, Doberman pinscher, Rottweiler, or German shepherd. You decide not to tell your insurer about your new Rottweiler/shepherd mix puppy. Should the dog bite a letter carrier, the party responsible for paying any damages is*

    b) you because you didn't inform the insurance carrier

GUIDE TO RESPONSIBLE DOG OWNERSHIP

Topic 1 / Lesson 2

4. *According to the American Veterinary Medical Association and the American Academy of Pediatrics, who are the most frequent victims of aggressive dogs?*

   d) Children

5. *In 2012, which city had the highest number of dog bite incidents involving mail carriers?*

   a) Los Angeles, CA

6. *Who assumes responsibility for medical bills and other expenses when a dog bites a mail carrier?*

   b) The dog owner

7. *What can the Postal Service do if your dog threatens and/or bites a mail carrier?*

   a) Discontinue delivery services until the situation is resolved.

Topic 1 / Lesson 3

8. b) At Large

9. b) Two, 36 month

10. a) 6 feet

Topic 3 / Lesson 1

11. **True**. *Male and female dogs will stop advertising their mating availability once they are spayed or neutered.*

12. **False**. *Behaviors that are rooted in other causes, such as fear or territorial reactions, need to be controlled through socialization and training.*

13. **True** *because the dog would be calmer and not feel the need to behave aggressively towards other dogs.*

14. **False**. *A spayed or neutered dog will not be driven to advertise its presence to potential mates and will mark its surroundings less often.*

Topic 3/ Lesson 2

15. *Worldwide bats are the most common source of human infection.* **False**

16. *In 2003 there were 52 rabies cases in the United States.* **False**

17. *Per California's health and safety code dogs must be vaccinated at* **3 months of age.**

Topic 1-3 Quiz

18. *If a dog injures another person, the dog owner could be liable*

    a) just because he is the owner and the dog bit someone under a state with statutory liability laws

    b) if he had previous knowledge of the dog's propensity to bite

    c) if he was negligent, for example by letting the dog off leash in a public place

    d) **all of the above**

19. *People most likely to be bit are*

    a) dog owners

    b) **children**

    c) Postal Carriers

    d) Veterinarians

20. *One very basic way to prevent dog bites is to*

    a) **keep a dog on a leash when in public**

    b) visit dog parks so the dog gets too tired to become aggressive

    c) only get a dog that is of a calm breed

    d) keep the dog in the house at all times

21. *A dog's temperament is determined by*

    a) breed

    b) genetics

    c) training and socialization

    d) **a combination of breed, genetics, training, and socialization**

22. *Aside from being a legal requirement, rabies vaccinations also*

    a) calm down the dog

    b) **protect people and the dog if it is bitten by a rabid animal**

    c) help in the dog's socialization

    d) repel wild animals who have rabies

23. *Neutering or spaying a dog is a good idea because it*

    a) controls aggressive behavior that is caused by the dog's need to mate

    b) reduces its willingness to roam to find a mate

    c) reduces its need to urinate to advertise its presence

    d) **all of the above**

Topic 4 / Lesson 2

24. *In which of these situations is the dog acting in a territorial manner:*

    a) The dog growls at you when you move its food bowl away while it is eating

    b) You walk by a house and a dog runs up to the fence and barks at you

    c) Your friend's dog growls at you when you are lifting up her infant son

    d) **All of the above**

25. *Which one of these situations exemplifies <u>proper</u> handling?*

    a) A person sneaks up on the dog from behind and pulls its ears

    b) **A person approaches the dog from the front, lets it sniff his hand, and pets him on the back**

    c) A person yanks a dog by its collar

    d) A person making loud noises runs up to the dog and tries to pet it

26. Which of these situations could make a dog afraid?

   a) Being in new surroundings with people it doesn't know

   b) A visit to the vet

   c) Loud construction work in front of the house

   d) **All of the above**

27. Which one of these situations are examples of rough play?

   a) Letting the dog grab your sleeve with its mouth and tugging it back and forth

   b) Wrestling with the dog on the floor

   c) Playing tug-of-war with a toy

   d) **All of the above**

Topic 4 Final Quiz

28. A dog displaying a closed mouth revealing the front teeth, with half-moon eyes, ears laid back against its head, its tail between its legs, and a cowering body posture is most likely feeling

   a) friendly

   b) angry

   c) **anxious**

29. An anxious dog is

   a) **dangerous because it could become so fearful that it decides to defend itself and bites the source of its fear**

   b) safe because it is too scared to do anything

   c) a good pack leader because it will make all decisions in a calm manner

30. When an unknown person runs up to a dog and makes loud noises, the dog will feel

   a) annoyed

   b) anxious

   c) challenged

   d) all of the above

31. The best time to socialize a dog is when it is

   a) 3-12 weeks old because the dog is willing to accept new experiences

   b) 4-6 months old after it's received all its vaccinations

   c) fully grown because it is less distractible than a puppy

32. When you socialize a dog you should

   a) immediately expose it to the whole of human society; dogs are resilient and can handle large crowds

   b) gradually, but steadily introduce the dog to new sounds, objects, and people

   c) keep it mostly at home because otherwise it will become too anxious

33. A dog questions your position as pack leader when

   a) it growls when you remove its food bowl

   b) charges through the door before you go

   c) bumps your hand while you are having dinner to get something to eat

   d) all of the above

34. When a person is the pack leader, the dog is

   a) resentful because the dog wants this position of power

   b) sad because it has to do what you tell it to

   c) calm because it knows its place in the hierarchy and is happy to follow your lead

Topic 6 / Lesson 1

35. What is the first thing you should do when your dog attacks or injures someone?

    a) Call 911

    b) Pull the victim away from your dog

    c) Pull your dog away from the victim and confine it if possible

    d) Pretend it's not your dog

Feedback: The first thing you need to do is to remove and secure your dog so it can't further injure the victim or hurt anyone else.

36. Once you've removed your dog, what should you do next?

    a) Call your vet to check on your dog's rabies information

    b) Assist the victim and contact emergency services if necessary

    c) Check on your dog to make sure it's okay

    d) Call your insurance agent

Feedback: Before you do anything else you have to assist the victim. Depending on the severity of the injury, the victim may need an ambulance.

37. What information should you give to the victim?

    a) Your name, address, and contact information

    b) Your dog's rabies vaccination date and dog license number

    c) Your veterinarian's information

    d) All of the above

Topic 5 and 6 Final Quiz

True/False Questions

38. To keep a dog from escaping it is best to have it chained in the yard. **False**

39. The only thing a dog needs in a yard is shade. **False**

40. There should always be fresh water available to a dog kept outdoors. **True**

Multiple Choice

41. The 10-day quarantine rule means

    a) when you first bring a dog home, it has to stay indoors for 10 days

    b) after a rabies vaccination, a dog has to stay home for 10 days

    c) if a dog bites someone, it has to be quarantined for 10 days to determine whether it has rabies

    d) after receiving your application for a dog license, it takes 10 days for the license to be issued

Sequencing
Put these steps in the right order.

42. When your dog is involved in a dog attack and injures a person, you should

- assist the victim **(2)**
- provide your personal information and your dog's information **(3)**
- remove your dog and confine it **(1)**
- gather the names and numbers of any witnesses **(4)**

ENDNOTES

1 Hoff, G.L., J. Cai, R. Kendrick, and R. Archer. "Emergency department visits and hospitalizations resulting from dog bites, Kansas City, MO, 1982-2002." Missouri Medicine 102 (2005): 565-568.

2 Meints, Kerstin and Tiny de Keuster. "Brief Report: Don't Kiss a Sleeping Dog: The First Assessment of ' The Blue Dog' Bite Prevention Program." Journal of Pediatric Psychology 34, no. 10 (2009): 1084-1090. http://dx.doi.org/10.1093/jpepsy/jsp053

3 Holmquist, Laurel and Anne Elixhauser. "Emergency Department Visits and Inpatient Stays Involving Dog Bites, 2008." Agency for Healthcare Research and Quality. November 2010. http://www.hcup-us.ahrq.gov/reports/statbriefs/sb101.pdf

4 Overall, Karen L. and Molly Love. "Dog Bites to Humans – Demography, Epidemiology, Injury and Risk." Journal of the American Veterinary Medical Association 218, no. 12 (2001): 1923-1933. http://dx.doi.org/10.2460/javma.2001.218.1923

5 Langley, Ricky L. "Human Fatalities Resulting from Dog Bite Attacks in the United States, 1979-2005." Wilderness and Environmental Medicine 20 (2009): 19-25. doi: 10.1580/08-WEME-OR-213.1.

6 Sacks, Jeffrey J., Leslie Sinclair, Julie Gilchrist, Gail C. Golab, and Randall Lockwood. "Breeds of Dogs Involved in Fatal Human Attacks in the United States between 1979 and 1998. Journal of the American Veterinary Medical Association 217, No. 6 (2000): 835-840. http://dx.doi.org/10.2460/javma.2000.217.836

7 "National Dog Bite Prevention Week: May 19-25, 2012." USPS Postal Bulletin Release No. PB 22336. May 3, 2012. http://about.usps.com/postal-bulletin/2012/pb22336/pdf/pb22336.pdf

8 "Postal Service Announces Top Dog Attack Cities." United States Postal Service, Release No. 11-050. May 12, 2011. http://about.usps.com/news/national-releases/2011/pr11_050.htm

9 "National Dog Bite Prevention Week: May 19-25, 2012."

10 Wisch, Rebecca F. "Table of State Leash Laws." Animal Legal & Historical Center: Michigan State University College of Law (2012). http://animallaw.info/articles/State%20Tables/tbusdogleash.htm

11 California Food and Agricultural Code: Division 14. Regulation and Licensing of Dogs: Chapter 9. Potentially Dangerous and Vicious Dogs - Article 1. Findings, Definitions, and General Provisions - Sections 31601-31609. http://doglaw.hugpug.com/law/california/31601-31609.html

12 "Dog Bite Myths Addressed." Christensen & Hymas Law Firm. http://www.utahpersonalinjurylawfirm.com/2012/11/dog-bite-myths-addressed/

13 Hoff, G.L., J. Cai, R. Kendrick, and R. Archer. "Emergency department visits and hospitalizations resulting from dog bites, Kansas City, MO, 1982-2002." Missouri Medicine 102 (2005): 565-568.

14 Meints, Kerstin and Tiny de Keuster. "Brief Report: Don't Kiss a Sleeping Dog: The First Assessment of "The Blue Dog" Bite Prevention Program." Journal of Pediatric Psychology 34, no. 10 (2009): 1084-1090. http://dx.doi.org/10.1093/jpepsy/jsp053

15 Holmquist, Laurel and Anne Elixhauser. "Emergency Department Visits and Inpatient Stays Involving Dog Bites, 2008." Agency for Healthcare Research and Quality. November 2010. http://www.hcup-us.ahrq.gov/reports/statbriefs/sb101.pdf

16 Overall, Karen L. and Molly Love. "Dog Bites to Humans – Demography, Epidemiology, Injury and Risk." Journal of the American Veterinary Medical Association 218, no. 12 (2001): 1923-1933. http://dx.doi.org/10.2460/javma.2001.218.1923

17 Langley, Ricky L. "Human Fatalities Resulting from Dog Bite Attacks in the United States, 1979-2005." Wilderness and Environmental Medicine 20 (2009): 19-25. doi: 10.1580/08-WEME-OR-213.1.

18 Sacks, Jeffrey J., Leslie Sinclair, Julie Gilchrist, Gail C. Golab, and Randall Lockwood. "Breeds of Dogs Involved in Fatal Human Attacks in the United States between 1979 and 1998. Journal of the American Veterinary Medical Association 217, No. 6 (2000): 835-840. http://dx.doi.org/10.2460/javma.2000.217.836

19 Swallow, Marguerite. "Dog Bites Claims: Insurers Have a Bone to Pick." Claims Magazine (2010). http://www.propertycasualty360.com/2010/12/01/dog-bite-claims-

20 "A Community Approach to Dog Bite Prevention." Veterinary Medicine Today: Canine Aggression Task Force. Journal of the American Veterinary Medical Association 218, no. 11 (2001): 1732-1749.

21 "National Dog Bite Prevention Week: May 19-25, 2012." USPS Postal Bulletin Release No. PB 22336. May 3, 2012. http://about.usps.com/postal-bulletin/2012/pb22336/pdf/pb22336.pdf

22 "Postal Service Announces Top Dog Attack Cities." United States Postal Service, Release No. 11-050. May 12, 2011. http://about.usps.com/news/national-releases/2011/pr11_050.htm

23 "National Dog Bite Prevention Week: May 19-25, 2012."

24 American Pet Products Manufacturers Association. 2007/2008 APPMA National Pet Survey. Greenwich, CT: American Pet Products Manufacturers Association; 2008.

25 "Human Fatalities Resulting from Dog Bite Attacks in the United States, 1979-2005," p. 24.

26 Sacks, Jeffrey J., Leslie Sinclair, Julie Gilchrist, Gail C. Golab, and Randall Lockwood. "Breeds of Dogs Involved in Fatal Human Attacks in the United States between 1979 and 1998. Journal of the American Veterinary Medical Association 217, No. 6 (2000): 835-840. http://dx.doi.org/10.2460/javma.2000.217.836

27 "Felony or Misdemeanor for Injury by Dangerous Dog." http://dogbitelaw.com/criminal-penalties-for-dog-bites/felony-or-misdemeanor-for-injury-by-dangerous-dog.html

28 Wisch, Rebecca F. "Table of State Leash Laws." Animal Legal & Historical Center: Michigan State University College of Law (2012). http://animallaw.info/articles/State%20Tables/tbusdogleash.htm

29 California Food and Agricultural Code: Division 14. Regulation and Licensing of Dogs: Chapter 9. Potentially Dangerous and Vicious Dogs - Article 1. Findings, Definitions, and General Provisions - Sections 31601-31609. http://doglaw.hugpug.com/law/california/31601-31609.html

30 Brown, Clark. "Are You a Leash Law Violator?" December 12, 2012. http://petsinceducationserv.ipage.com/wp/understanding-us/

31 California Civil Code Section 3342 & 3342.5. http://www.leginfo.ca.gov/cgi-bin/displaycode?section=civ&group=03001-04000&file=3333-3343.7

32 "A Negligent Dog Owner's Liability." NOLO: Law for All. http://www.nolo.com/legal-encyclopedia/a-negligent-dog-owners-liability.html

33 "Which are the One Bite States?" Dog Bite Law. http://dog-bitelaw.com/faq/which-are-the-one-bite-states.html

34 "Dog Bite Myths Addressed." Christensen & Hymas Law Firm. http://www.utahpersonalinjurylawfirm.com/2012/11/dog-bite-myths-addressed/

35 "Dog Bite Prevention." American Veterinary Medical Association (2010). https://ebusiness.avma.org/ebusiness50/files/productdownloads/dog_bite_brochure.pdf

36 "A Community Approach to Dog Bite Prevention," p. 1740. "Prevent Your Dog From Biting." The Humane Society of the United States. July 30, 2010. http://www.humanesociety.org/animals/dogs/tips/prevent_dog_bites.html

37 "Dog Bite Prevention," p. 3.

38 http://www.kgwn.tv/home/headlines/Rare-Human-Rabies-Case-Confirmed-in-Fremont-County-Resident- 330472301.html

39 http://www.startribune.com/wyoming-sees-first-confirmed-human-case-of-rabies/330508511/

40 http://www.nydailynews.com/news/national/wyo-woman-rabies-human-state-disease-article-1.2384011

41 http://www.cdc.gov/rabies/location/usa/surveillance/human_rabies.html

42 http://www.who.int/rabies/about/en/

43 http://www.nature.com/scitable/blog/viruses101/is_rabies_really_100_fatal 44http://www.cdc.gov/rabies/prevention/index.html

45 http://www.who.int/rabies/about/en/

46 Maltese: I Just Got a Puppy, What Do I Do? by Mordecai Siegal, Matthew Margolis, and Tara Darling, Simon and Schuster, 2002.

47 Planet dog: a doglopedia by Harry Choron, Houghton Mifflin, 2005.

Puppy Parenting: Everything You Need to Know About Your Puppy's First Year by Jan Greye, Gail Smith, and Beverly Beyette, Harper Collins, 2002.

Bianco, Jay. "Separation Anxiety". Maltese Only. Retrieved 14 July 2012.

48 Beagle: Fogle pp.176–7

49 Rough Collie: "Collie Breed Standard". American Kennel Club. 1977-05-10. Retrieved 2008-02-08.

"Collie (Rough) Breed Standard". The Kennel Club. 2006-05-12. Retrieved 2008-02-08.

50 German Shepherd: "German Shepherd Dog Breed Standard". American Kennel Club.

"Breed Standard — German Shepherd". New Zealand Kennel Club. Retrieved 19 July 2008. "While the dog should be approachable and friendly, he does not make immediate friendships with strangers."

Dogwise: The Natural way to Train your Dog (1992), John Fisher Souvenir Press Ltd. ISBN 0-285-63114-4

51 Rottweiler: "Get to Know the Rottweiler", 'The American Kennel Club', Retrieved 29 May 2014

www.ingramcontent.com/pod-product-compliance
Lightning Source LLC
Chambersburg PA
CBHW060317240426
43661CB00059B/2794